BEING EXTRAORDINARY

How to Live Life on Purpose

IAN LOCK

Edited by Anni Townend

lıp

First published in 2013 by:
Live It Publishing
27 Old Gloucester Road
London, United Kingdom.
WC1N 3AX
www.liveitpublishing.com

Printed in UK, USA & Australia by Lightning Source

978-1-906954-70-3 (pbk)
978-1-906954-71-0 (ebk)

contents

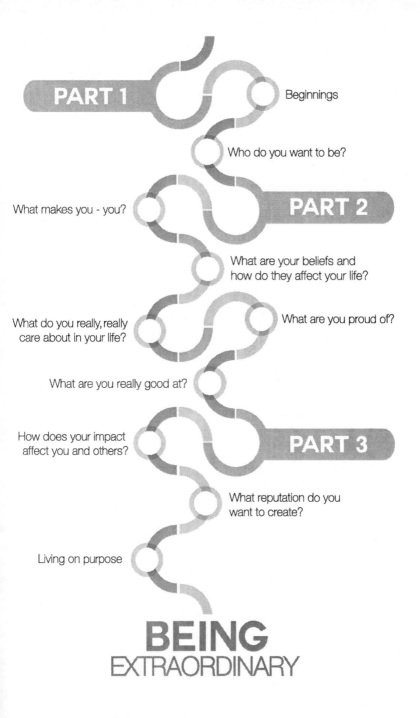

PART 1 — Beginnings

Who do you want to be?

What makes you - you? — PART 2

What are your beliefs and how do they affect your life?

What do you really, really care about in your life?

What are you proud of?

What are you really good at?

How does your impact affect you and others? — PART 3

What reputation do you want to create?

Living on purpose

BEING
EXTRAORDINARY

what is freedom?

maybe it's the ability to choose to be you
and live the life you want.

if so, it's available to us all
and that's the choice.

preface

I am delighted to be writing a preface to this great book written by my colleague and friend, Ian Lock. There are very few books that do what they say they do! This book does. It will help you find your purpose, what really matters to you and to live your life fully. It will help you make the difference that you want, to who you are, wherever you are. Ian takes you on a journey into your life, to finding your true purpose. He shares his own experience, his successes and failures, and what he has learnt from them and from others.

It is some years ago that he and I first talked about writing a series of books together; inspired not only by our work as leadership consultants but also by our shared love of walking and in particular our each looking after a 4 mile stretch of the South Downs Way in Sussex. It was after sharing one of these walks that we got talking, around the kitchen table, about the series of books that we wanted to write.

Ian believes that people can be more than they are and he brings this passion and commitment to everyone. He walks alongside you offering his knowledge and experience, playing with ideas, challenging thinking and encouraging new and different ways of feeling that have us be more of ourselves. Ian asks great questions that have you stop and think, and take a look at where you are standing and what might be possible if you stood in a different place, a place of possibility and purpose.

Being Extraordinary takes you on a journey that feels like going for a walk and talk together, as you would with a friend. It feels like having a conversation, asking questions, sharing some stories, and sometimes pointing things out by way of choices, possibilities, or things that you had noticed. It's as if Ian is by your side having a conversation with you, occasionally nudging you along, sometimes sharing his own experience and other times encouraging you to reflect upon your own experience and journey. He encourages you to walk further, to climb higher and to explore new ground.

This book is a powerful guide to anyone who wants more from their life – read it! Go on and be extraordinary!

Anni Townend, Summer 2012

Today is different,

today has possibilities whereas yesterday had none.

Yesterday I thought I was a free spirit, drifting on the ocean

going wherever the wind and tide would take me.

Today I am free.

I am no longer drifting, the sails are taut, the boat is heeled

over and I am sailing in a direction of my own choosing with

the wind and spray of life in my face.

Real freedom is not drifting aimlessly,

freedom is setting a course, having a reason and meaning,

freedom is moving forward on purpose.

Today is my beginning

beginnings

PART 1

Beginnings

Who do you want to be?

In the beginning there was you and the world was full of wonder. You have always had the option to shape your life and choose how you are going to live it. You still do.

chapter 1

beginnings

This book takes you on a journey that will help you feel good about who you are, how you behave and explore your purpose. It will also give you a great perspective to use in approaching all the situations you face in your life. This will help you to be better and more successful at everything you want to do. Underpinning all of this, Being Extraordinary can help you to be happy more of the time and spend more time being you and enjoying who that is – whatever you are choosing to do.

When we know what we stand for and why, we can make choices based upon that. When we are living our life in the way that we want to, being true to ourselves and aspiring to do something that is important to us and that we care about, we feel different. We feel like we're involved in something that is bigger than the daily routine and that feeds our energy rather than drains it. When we are connected to a purpose it can bring a very different feeling of being alive.

Within the following pages is a guide that will help you to create your route to living the life that you want and to being the person that you want to be. As you read through Being Extraordinary, the perspectives and questions you explore are creating the foundation for you to produce your guide for your life. It will all come together at the end.

There are very few guarantees in this life or in this book. One that I will make is that if you follow this simple guide it will change things and make a difference. Read the book and follow the guidelines that you create for 28 days. Just by investing that time I'd be very surprised if things were not already starting to feel very different for you.

To start with, much of what you are exploring here is not about having a 'brilliant' answer and it is certainly not about trying to 'get it right'. The theme throughout is ease and exploration so I am encouraging you to read the stories, perspectives and questions from a place of open minded wonder. Whatever your thoughts are as you read, play with them and see what you can create, just let it flow.

What you notice as you read on is a really good source of information for you. Notice how any of the stories, perspectives, quotes or questions make you feel, and then just ask yourself what that might be telling you about you. The whole idea of the book is to provoke and stimulate your thoughts and feelings, so any reaction is a good one! If anything I've written makes you happy, sad, cross, indignant or anything else, maybe go back and read that bit again with the question – 'Why am I feeling like this?' and note how your beliefs, experiences and opinions are helping you or getting in the way. Remember as you read the book that any reactions are not hardwired into your head, all of them have been informed by the life you've lived so far. As you adapt your approach and beliefs to ones that are more in keeping with your true self, you will start to notice different things.

In my experience your intuition will guide you. Wherever it leads you first is normally a large part of your true self, don't spend too much time analysing. There are questions throughout and their purpose is to stimulate thinking and help you collect your hopes and thoughts. Some of the questions appear in the text as part of the conversation and others are in boxes. They are there for you to pause and think about and you could make notes as you go or wait until the end of the chapter, whichever way works best for you. If you want to get started right away there are several blank pages at the end of each chapter for your thoughts.

There are no right or wrong answers to any of the areas explored in the book. There are no answers that you should or ought to have. There are only your answers and if they sit well with you then that's all that matters.

Enjoy your journey.

who do you want to be?

Many years ago someone asked me 'who do you want to be'? My initial thinking took me to who in the world would I be if I could. At that time I admired people like Nelson Mandela, Bob Geldof and my good friend Jo. They all had a sense of purpose and values to guide them, appeared to be principled and had no trouble calling the world the way they saw it – people who represented things I would like to be true of me. This gave me an insight into the question 'who do you want to be?' and started me on a journey of purpose that is ongoing. In essence I have interpreted the question as this – If you could appear in any way in the world, if you could choose to be at your best, if you could have the impact on those around that you truly wanted to have – what would that person be like, how would they appear in the world, what life might they create for themselves and others? Now that, I thought, is a question worth answering.

Over the years I have sought a way to help myself and others answer this question and contained within these pages is the most simple and powerful method I have discovered of bringing this to life.

When we are young we are able to choose many times a day who we are going to be. These are often flights of fancy and they do show a remarkable ability that we have to choose to be someone or something. When I was little it was often a soldier or a superhero or an astronaut. How about you?

As we grow older we can get stuck in 'this is who I am and that's it' whereas there is always a whole rich world out there that is still waiting for us to choose. I really believe that you can be whoever you want to be at any time in your life, as long as whoever you choose to be reflects who you really are at your core. If that person has your values and beliefs and cares about and acts upon them you can be genuine and authentic. This isn't asking you to be someone else or to look at another's life and say I wish I was them. The question 'Who do you want to be?' is directed at you and really means 'Who is the person that you want to be?'

If you could be anyone, who would you be?

I often meet people who tell me the person they want to be is different at work than at home, they have a different set of values and beliefs that they bring to different situations. I remember spending time with someone who argued that their behaviour at work was completely justifiable because their job needed them to be dictatorial and aggressive to get the work done and that some fear in their employees was good. When I asked if they would behave that way at home or apply that thinking to their children or their partner, they replied that they'd never get away with it and anyway it wouldn't be appropriate to treat your family like that! It was only as they were saying it that you could see the realisation dawning on them, that it wasn't really appropriate to behave like that anywhere. We seem to get stuck in the belief that the end justifies the means. It rarely does and it's a great excuse for us to hide behind. Usually behaviour that doesn't reflect our true self comes from a desire to be successful and look good. In fact our poor behaviours often come out when we feel what we hold most dear at our core, our values and beliefs, are being threatened in some way. Strangely enough our poor behaviours never get us what we really want.

Thinking about who we want to be helps us to plot a course to steer our life from. It allows us to be clear on what we care about and actively describe how we will appear in the world. It stops us slipping into our reactive, survival behaviour and allows us to handle all of our life as the person we would choose to be. I often find myself asking how the best me would handle a situation as opposed to the reactive me who is just trying to survive the moment.

When you are at your best, how do you handle things?

What's the result?

When I reflect back on my life there are many situations where I have not behaved well and where I used anything as an excuse to justify my behaviour. For some I can still prove to you that I won or had the outcome I was looking for. In truth I only survived and that, for me, is not enough. When I'm reacting to a situation or just trying to survive it, I need to be seen as good at what I am doing and I usually need to be right. I am not paying attention to my impact or its effect on others and my behaviour is generally uninspiring to say the least. When I am being true to myself I want to feel proud of the way I handled a situation, I want to be able to look at myself in the mirror at the end of the day and feel great about how I behaved. Feelings of anger and righteousness never make me feel good and even if they do in that moment they rarely create anything positive for me. Choosing who you really are and being clear on who you want to be can give you a great rock to stand on as you move through your life. Whoever said that you have to accept your life as it is, was wrong.

The place to start any journey from is always where you are right now with your hopes, dreams and aspirations for the future. At the heart of any dream for the future is the person you were born to be. The person who always comes out to play when the sun is shining and you are happy. This version of you often views the world as a place full of hope and possibility. The start of this journey is exploring who that person is and how they inhabit the world. Once you're clear on that you can begin to shape everything around you.

How would you want to describe yourself at your best?

When you are at your best, what are the qualities that you have?

The other side of this coin is who you don't want to be. I'll not spend too much time on this subject in Being Extraordinary, save to say that it's very useful to make a list of all the behaviours you have that you associate with the person you don't want to be. This is just so you can recognise that person when they're knocking at the door. For me that person can be a little aggressive, uncaring, selfish, concerned with looking good, needy, domineering, controlling and unhealthily competitive. He tends to appear when I'm feeling small and need to be in survival mode. He is normally only concerned with getting through the next few minutes or hours. He is never consciously concerned about the future or what I really care about in the world. This part of me is brilliant at what he does – he tends to cause a 'disruption to' or a 'lessening of' just about everything that is important to me. He appears when I perceive that what really matters to me is being threatened. Notice I say perceive, because it usually isn't being threatened, I am just seeing the world from that perspective in the moment.

Who do you not want to be?

What situations bring this person out?

How does it feel to be this person and how do you recognise them?

who do you want to be?

notes

what makes
you – you?

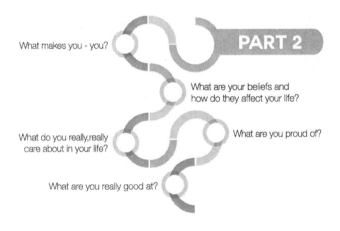

What makes you - you?

PART 2

What are your beliefs and
how do they affect your life?

What do you really, really
care about in your life?

What are you proud of?

What are you really good at?

Throughout history we have always tried

to tell one story in everything that we do.

That story is –

'Who am I?'

what makes you – you?

There is something at our core that shapes who we are and everything we do. Much of it is based on past experience and without having another choice to make we are great at unconsciously allowing our past to automatically shape our actions in the present or the future. This can sound complicated and needn't be. My approach to this is to focus on the present and the future and to choose from there how we are going act.

What makes us – us, are our values, beliefs and what we care about and this sets up how we interact with the world. With practice and focus we can learn to use what's important to us to help ourselves and others achieve great things in life.

Without conscious clarity on what is at our core, how can we choose how we will behave at any given moment? What will guide us to be the person that we are aspiring to be? How can we change anything if what we are doing is based on reaction and not choice, or we don't know what or why we want to change?

Our behavioural reactions can often be based on unconscious learning from an earlier part of our life. For example an aggressive or controlling or defensive reaction may have served us well, back in the distant past and we tend to recycle these behaviours as an unconscious response to a similar situation that we find ourselves in. However, what we needed when we learnt these reactions may not be necessary anymore. For instance as a child we may have needed to do what we were told, surrender to someone else's authority, react aggressively or defensively. As adults we are able to have a much healthier interaction with whatever situation we are facing. Sometimes our unconscious reactions achieve our desired outcome in the way that we want and at other times they can have much more serious consequences. This is not wrong, it is just our old survival mechanism doing what it does best, helping us to survive in the only way it has learnt how to.

What are some of your unconscious reactions to situations?

Which of them don't help and which are useful?

As we move forward in our lives, increasing our consciousness around who we want to be and the life we want to live on purpose, it is possible and necessary to address and sometimes change these unconscious learnings when they are not helping to create the life that we want. This approach lets us look to the future and to our aspirations to choose how we want to behave. To do that we need to choose what our start point is, we need to start with what is at the very heart of us that underpins our life.

what do you stand for?

The place to start defining what we really care about is with our values. A value is a principle that underpins our lives and can be anything that we want it to be. Our values can be said to provide us with energy and light, and therefore they remind us of what we are truly about and give us a clarity of direction. Values are often described by words like honesty, integrity, trust, love, fun, happiness, equality and respect. The list of available values is endless. It doesn't matter what you choose for your values as long as they are really important to you. I have often thought that they can be accessed by thinking about how you would most like your children or your friends and colleagues to be impacted by the way you behave and interact on a daily basis. They will flow through everything you feel, think, say and do. Our values are so important to us that, at our best, we will often go to great lengths to have them recognised and protected.

Over the years I have asked the question 'What are your values that guide you?' to thousands of people and leaders all over the world. Over 95% of them have found the question a challenging one at first because they have not explored this for a very long time, if ever!

It doesn't mean they're not there, it just means that we're not conscious of them or acting consciously from them. It's not enough to identify what our values are, we have to be clear on what they mean for us and how we interpret them. My top three values are honesty, integrity and respect.

Honesty. For me it is about being straight. It is about never telling an untruth to benefit or advantage myself in a situation. It is about finding the courage to be honest when traditional survival might encourage me to be false. It is about speaking my truth and being true to myself. It is not about saying what's on my mind at any given moment, or telling everyone what I think of them all the time, it is not about forcing my honesty upon the world.

Integrity. For me it means that you can always count on me to do what I say I am going to do. I will keep my word and if, for whatever reason, I am unable to I will own it and not try to hide and I will come and talk to you about it. It means that I will aspire to act within my values and beliefs whether I succeed or fail.

Respect. To treat myself and others with respect means that I try to understand who they are and what they are doing. It is about being genuinely interested in a different point of view. It means that I want to find out about others and understand the world from their experience. It means whatever you do, even if I disagree with it and it causes conflict, I want to handle it with respect.

What values do you stand for?

What do they mean to you?

How did they appear in your life today?

Notice what you're thinking now about your values, do you act according to them on a daily basis or are they negotiable?

what makes
you – you?

notes

what are your beliefs and how do they affect your life?

Beliefs are so important to us in our life. What we believe shapes how we behave, what we expect, our sense of possibility in the world and most importantly our level of happiness and fulfilment. Quite often our beliefs sit just below our level of consciousness and shape our interaction with life. Of course we regularly behave as if our beliefs are universal truths as well, rather than what they are, just beliefs. Think of some beliefs you have about the world you live in or people that you know. How many of them are universally true and how many of them are just true to you? How often do you act as if they are the truth? Now you may be able to find others in the world who share those beliefs and that may make you feel better about them. It doesn't change the fact that they're still only beliefs. What I am asking you to do here is create some positive beliefs about the world and the people in it. These wont be '*the truth'* either and they will help you arrive in the world the way that you want to.

What you focus on becomes your reality, so focus on something good that is positive and see what happens

This again is aspirational, think of it as the beliefs that you want to hold about you and the world that will help and support who you want to be.

Here are some of mine:

1. I believe that everyone is born brilliant and wonderful and that many of us are very good at hiding that behind some unpleasant behaviours and actions that would suggest otherwise. If I were to take everyone I meet at face value I would have missed some truly great and inspiring people over the years. Now is this belief true? Not always. Will I meet some people who are not wonderful underneath it all? Possibly (although I haven't yet in the last 15 years). Is there

a risk to this belief? Yes. People may try to take advantage of my good nature. Is it worth it? Absolutely. Because it helps me to be who I want to be. This belief helps me to see others as great people and helps them to find that for themselves.

2. I believe that you have the answers to your life, your problems and your success. This requires me to interact with you in a way that starts with this in mind and encourages you to explore your world and your life. It stops me from trying to tell you what to do. It helps me do the same with my life.

3. I believe that I am a good man who is able to make a difference in the world. I believe that I do a good job and that I am someone worth knowing. This belief helps me to live my life and be who I want to be. It gives me the self belief to attempt the extraordinary.

4. I believe that I and others are better than we truly think we are. With time to stop and really look at ourselves we can see what difference we can make to our lives and the world that we live in. This helps me to always look for the possibilities in others and myself.

5. I believe that I have real potential and that the world is full of potential. That human beings can create a society that has room for all and caters for huge diversity of interests, beliefs, aspirations and cultures. I believe that with dialogue, understanding and conversation we find most of us are not very far apart in our fundamental ideology, hope and ambitions. This belief really helps me to maintain my sense of purpose, especially when life gets tough.

6. I believe that I can make a difference and influence the life that I am living. This means that at my best, I don't accept what life throws at me if it doesn't fit with the world I want to live in. It helps me believe that I can change things and that it is worth the commitment and effort that I put into my life.

The important point here is that none of my beliefs are true, even though they are positive. I have them because they help me be who I want to be. They help me see the world in a way that encourages me to be positive and they do create possibilities for me and others.

What positive and powerful beliefs would you like to hold about you and the world you live in that will help you?

How will they impact on and in your life?

It helps here to let your values guide your beliefs and remember they are aspirational so you can choose any beliefs that you want.

Be bold and write some great beliefs about you and your world.

Now consider some of the beliefs you hold about yourself and the world you live in that are not helpful or are even destructive for you. Beliefs that cause you to behave in a way that isn't you at your best. Have a think about what they are and how they can affect the way you act and feel.

Here are some of my unhelpful and destructive beliefs:

1. I can wrongly believe that I'm a victim. That the world conspires to make my life difficult and there is

nothing I can do about it. That I am powerless to change things and I have to accept what I am given. This belief makes me small and ends up making me a cross and angry person to be around. I don't attempt to make a difference or change my life when I believe this and feel that the world is against me.

2. I can wrongly believe that I'm not good enough. That anything I try will be found wanting and will probably go wrong. That I'm not good enough at my job, as a father and husband and at some point this will become obvious to others. This belief again makes me small and puts me into a survival mode where I don't choose my behaviour, I just react.

3. I can wrongly believe that I'm going to be found out. That at some point everyone around me will discover that I have been bluffing my way through whatever I am doing. This belief wears me out because it makes me spend lots of time trying to prove to others that it is not true.

4. I can wrongly believe that you can't change who you are, it's hardwired into you, just accept it. This belief

allows me to say terrible cliches to people like ' you'll have to take me as I am, warts and all – I can't change it – you either love me or hate me' It allows me to justify poor behaviour and doesn't represent who I want to be.

5. I can wrongly believe that you can't make a difference in the world. Well this one is simple, it stops me trying.

6. I can wrongly believe that everyone else is doing it so it must be alright. My great cry of self justification for littering, not recycling, smoking, drinking, accepting the rules of life that we are given, behaving poorly to a particular group of human beings, wasting food, spending money, driving too fast, walking by without doing anything and so on and so on. Fill in your own list here as appropriate.

These beliefs do not help in anyway, ever. I do sometimes choose to believe that they are true and they always have the impact on me that I have described. They do have one key thing in common, they de-energise me and reduce the possibilities for me and others in my life.

You do have a choice here! You can choose to believe they are true and accept the impact they have on your life or you can choose to see everything that they stop you from creating and practise getting rid of them.

*What beliefs do you hold that are
not helpful to you?*

How do they affect your life?

*What would be possible if you were
able to ignore them?*

self belief

For many of us our self belief is an important part of the way we view ourselves and the possibilities in our lives. Our self belief impacts upon everything that we are and everything that we do. People with true self belief can go anywhere and do anything. People with false self belief, or bravado, often just pretend they can.

Can you remember a time when you truly believed in yourself, felt good about who you were and what you could do? Even if it was only for a brief moment in time, can you remember how you felt and what you believed? At that moment in your life what was possible for you? What positive beliefs did you have? Imagine what it would be like to feel that more of the time. What would it be like to do with your life whatever you wanted?

That voice in your head might already be talking to you as you read this. Listen to it. What's it telling you about your self belief and the possibilities for your life? Notice if it's increasing your self belief or reducing it. Self belief helps us to say this is the life I'm living, this is the life I want to be living and here are some obstacles that are getting in the way, I wonder how I'm going to get around them. Lack of self belief changes our view and says this is me, I'm stuck, and here are all the good reasons why I can't change. The difference between us feeling powerful and powerless is all about our belief.

Believing in yourself doesn't guarantee that you will always succeed – but your energy will be different, how you feel will be different, your ability to handle everything that happens in your life will be different. Think back to a day or a time when you felt great and had real self belief. What did it feel like and how did you behave? What was possible?

Think about how you would want to be in the future with your really powerful self beliefs.

What words would you want to use to describe you?

How would you want to feel?

How will your new positive beliefs help you?

Choose anything you want – you can't get this wrong and some of your answers might even make you smile.

Once we're clear on what we want to believe, it can help to look at how we approach some of the choices and situations that we face in life. What we're believing at any time can seriously affect our thinking. When we are choosing to see everything from a negative place the possibilities all become a lot smaller and life can seem frightening or worrisome. When we are choosing to see ourselves and the world as a place full of possibility we have a very different attitude. Something I have learnt over the years is to listen to how I'm thinking about things. I often hear the voice in my head saying 'what if it doesn't work?', 'what will you do then?', 'don't risk it'. I work hard to replace these thoughts with 'what if it did work?', 'what would my life be like then?', 'give it a go.' It doesn't guarantee that what I am trying will work, although it does let me try in the first place. I have a great chance of making a difference with the 'powerful self belief' approach but no purposeful chance without it. There is a conversation in one of my earliest favourite books, Winnie the Pooh, which describes this wonderfully.

Pooh and Piglet were walking through the woods on a dark and stormy night where the wind was blowing hard through the trees. Piglet, a small and frightened animal, looked up at Pooh and said 'It is very windy Pooh, what if a tree falls on us?' Pooh thought for a while and looked down at Piglet and said 'What if it doesn't?'

It can help us to look at our lives from this perspective, what if it goes wrong or what if it doesn't? What if I fail or what if I don't? What if I can't change anything or what if I can? What if I try to change my life and make it worse or what if it was even better? What if a tree falls on me or what if it doesn't?

When I take Pooh's approach to worries and concerns I have more energy and purpose and I go out there and do things that help to create the life I want to live. When I take Piglet's approach I am a small and frightened animal and do nothing.

*What are some of the situations
that you face in your life?*

*How does it look from the
Pooh and Piglet perspective?*

*What happens if you approach these
things from your positive self belief?*

As you have read this chapter and thought about the questions, what did you notice about your answers? Is it easier for you to believe the positive about yourself and the world, or the negative and more importantly what impact does either have on the outcome? Whatever we notice is a good signpost to how we view the world as we walk through it. The important bit here is what do you want to believe and how will that help you, and if you do believe in yourself, what might be possible in your life? Now choose which beliefs will help you and practise focusing on them whenever you can – and when the negative beliefs arrive, recognise them, see them for what they are, just beliefs, and how they make you small, and then remind yourself of what you really want to believe.

Our deepest fear is not that we are inadequate.
Our deepest fear is that we are powerful beyond measure.
It is our light, not our darkness that most frightens us.
We ask ourselves:
Who am I to be brilliant, gorgeous, talented and fabulous?
Actually, who are you not to be?

By Marianne Willamson
Excerpt from Our Deepest Fear published in A Return to Love:
Reflections on the Principles of a "Course in Miracles"

what are your beliefs
and how do they
affect your life?

notes

chapter 5

what do you really, really
care about in your life?

What we care about underpins everything we do, say and feel. It is at the core of us and shapes our purpose whether we are clear on it or not. What we care about can cover many areas and can be beliefs, objects, people, philosophies and numerous other things. What is important here is that we are able to honestly articulate what we do care about.

Some of the things that I care about are:

- I care about my Family – Diane, Joshua, Roddy and Imogen are really important parts of my life. Without them much of what I do would be empty. With them present what I do is full and inspiring for me and others.
- I care about the weak and the helpless – This covers those who can't help themselves. People who are

hungry, mentally or physically ill or unstable, children especially and people who are miserable and unhappy and don't know why. The world I want to live in nurtures and helps these people and nobody goes to bed hungry or crying or feeling alone.

- I care about being thought well of – I care that others value me and want to have me around. This caring can sometimes make me needy and that doesn't help. At my best I still care what others think of me but it doesn't prevent me from being my best.

- I care about inspiring leadership – I believe the world can be populated by people who know what they care about and what their purpose is and who are prepared to go out and inspire others. Too often today we are beset by hoplessness and apathy and it's easy to succumb to whatever life throws at us. I care that we design our own lives and live with great purpose. I care that people see the magic of their own leadership whoever they are and whatever they do. I care that people are happy in whatever way they want to be.

What do you care about?

*What are the things that are important
to you in your life?*

What else would you really like to be on this list?

what do you really, really care about in your life?

notes

what are you proud of?

It is amazing how little time we spend reminding ourselves of the good and great achievements in our lives. Notice how quickly you had an answer to that question at the top of this paragraph. Notice what your inner voice said to you as you read it. For some an immediate list may spring to mind and for many of us this is, initially, a difficult question. I have yet to meet anyone who after some reflection couldn't see that there are accomplishments that they can be immensely proud of. We tend to at look our achievements and acomplishments and those of others, and see them as common place, therefore not worthy of our attention. There are the big challenges that human beings choose to take on, some of them classics. Mountains are climbed, oceans crossed, battles fought, depths plumbed, moons reached, foes vanquished, dragons slain and hearts won. These classics are all mirrored in smaller ways in our everyday lives and most days we are all doing some amazing things.

There is much we do that we could be proud of. For some it is having the courage to make an important decision, going seven days without smoking or drinking, becoming a parent, being a good friend to others or digging the garden. For others it is having the courage to ask that person out on a date, standing up for something you believe in, living true to your values and beliefs, having a really difficult conversation or doing something that traditionally has scared you. It could be significant events from your life, realtionships started, ended or sustained, exams passed, degrees or diplomas gained, sporting events, competitions entered, driving tests passed. Beyond this it could be those moments when you have chosen to walk into the fire or into the dark not knowing what the outcome would be and it feeling like the most terrifying thing you have ever done.

What are the things you've done in your life that make you feel great about you?

You might want to get some help on this one.

As I was finishing this book it was suggested to me that I should contact people I have worked with over the years and ask them to say a few words about my impact and the difference I have made. This was so I could help you, the reader, understand a bit more about me and the work that I do. I put this off for as long as possible because it just didn't feel comfortable, and what if there was nothing good to say. Even with a successful career behind me I was doubting that I had made a difference or done anything special. We often cannot see for ourselves that what we do is special. I have had some staggering conversations with people where someone who is struggling with this question will say " The only thing that springs to mind, and I'm not really proud of it is… I once saved someone's life by giving them CPR" True Story! He simply didn't think it was special and it didn't occur to him that this would make it to his list of things he was proud of. The voice in our heads often says, and notice if you ever say this, 'If I did it then it's probably not special!'

Some things that I'm proud of:

1. I am proud of my relationship with my family. I have my fantastic wife Diane, and our three great children Josh, Roddy and Imogen. I think I do well as a dad and a husband. I'm proud of the conversations that we all have to make our family work.

2. I am proud of my business and what I have accomplished. Although much of what I do scares me at times I am able to find the courage to do it. I am proud that what I do makes a big difference to the people I work with and the organisations they work in. I am really proud of the feedback that so many people were prepared to give and be put into print at the back of this book.

3. I am proud that I've had the courage to write this book. I've been talking about it for years and now it's happened. I'm even prouder that I've had the courage to publish it.

4. I am proud of who I have been for my family over the past two years. We have had several close family

members with serious illness and I have been able to be there for them and help them through some really tough times.

5. I am proud that I left my job to follow my dream. Leaving a safe job with all of the security that goes with it and entering a life of complete uncertainty and no guarantees was a real leap of faith.

Start to make a list of the things that you are proud of in your life. Ask some people close to you what they think you can be proud of...

What are you proud of?

When you are proud of yourself what are the words that you use?

What are you going to do today to add to this list?

What do you want to do in the coming weeks and months that will make you feel proud? It could be something for you or about you or for others. Write down some of the things. Why not go and do them.

what are you
proud of?

notes

what are you really good at?

Now here's a title that often makes people feel uncomfortable. We can live in a society that can focus on where we need to improve, what did not go well today or what I'm told I'm not very good at. This chapter helps you to look at what you are naturally good at. I've worked with lots of people on this question and I have never met anyone who is not good at something and invariably a whole variety of things. So why not take a quiet moment and start to think about everything that you do really well or that comes easily to you. You will have had this feedback all through your life whether you realise it or not. From school reports, appraisals at work or from what those in your life ask of you.

Look at all the different roles that you play in your life. Make a list of everything that you are good at. Find some good friends or family and ask them to tell you what they think is good and valuable about you – Come on – you've done this in the last chapter so go ask them again.

What are you really good at?

What is it about you that others value?

*What do you find yourself doing well? Are you
good at relationships, are you loyal, are you
trustworthy, are you a great driver, do you cook
well, can you paint etc?*

Again listen for that voice in your head as you think about asking others this question – if it's telling you not to do this then think long and hard – it's a good indicator that it might be lessening your self belief and ability to shape your own life in lots of different ways. Notice the difference here between your unhelpful inner voice and your helpful inner voice. Your unhelpful inner voice is probably scared or small and is reducing your ability to do what you want. It's probably telling you not to ask anyone else what you are good at. Your helpful inner voice is increasing your self belief and the amount of possibilities in your life. It's probably saying that this feels a little uncomfortable but why not give it a try. Which one are you going to choose to listen to?

Over the last 5 chapters we have been looking at our values, beliefs and what it is that we really care about. These underpin much of what we do and people often describe this within themselves as their core. It helps us to identify what is at our core so we can use it to help clarify the choices we make for our behaviours and our purpose. We have also looked at what we are proud of and the things that we are good at in order to remind ourselves of the possibilities that already exist in our lives.

what are you
really good at?

notes

being
extraordinary

How does your impact
affect you and others?

PART 3

What reputation do you
want to create?

Living on purpose

BEING
EXTRAORDINARY

There is no such thing as an ordinary

person, in fact it is impossible. Everyone

you've ever met is in some way

extraordinary

how does your impact affect you and others?

Something we're all really good at is having an impact. It's an ability we have just by being alive. Everything we do, and at times don't do, has an impact. Our impact can increase or reduce the possibilities around us and it can affect everything and everybody that we come into contact with. Our presence has an impact and our absence has an impact. What we say, what we feel, what we think, what we believe and what we want all have an impact. Having the impact that we want usually requires us to choose how we want others to feel around us and then pay attention to it. Once you start looking it can be easy to see the impact that we have. We usually notice the impact that others have on us by the way we feel when someone is saying or doing something around us. A great way to understand your own impact is to notice what happens around you – are people happy or sad? Do people want to talk to you?

Do people laugh around you? When you talk do people listen? When you listen do people talk? Do people notice you or are you invisible? Did someone's life change today because you were there? Did you make a difference today? Did you enjoy your life today?

What do you notice about the impact
you have at the moment?

When does it fit with your values and beliefs?

When I was a teenager I had absolutely no idea of the impact that I had on the world around me or the people who lived in it alongside me. My life was all about me, what I wanted, what was convenient for me. Everything I did was centred on what I thought I wanted and what I needed. I learnt quickly to bend the truth or even to lie to serve my own ends and I would do what I thought was right and hang the consequences. A few things happened that woke me up to my impact and the person I could have become.

I was sitting with a good friend and a group of people one evening and we were all talking about something important. I must have kept interrupting and wanting to put my point of view across which was obviously the most important one that everybody would want to hear! Eventually she turned to me and said 'What makes you think that what you have to say is so important that it can't wait for someone else to finish speaking, why don't you listen to what is being said, you might just learn something? When you do that you are being rude, you stop the conversation and what you have to say isn't always the most interesting thing.' For a while there I was in deep shock, no one had ever spoken to me like that, it was probably about time, and I felt very small. I had thought that what I was saying was the most important thing and I certainly wasn't thinking that I had anything to learn. I was in my late teens at the time and it's one of the best things anyone has ever said to me. It was also great feedback on the impact I was having.

When I was seventeen I joined a firm selling photocopiers. I was successful and even set up my own business in the same marketplace. The more I learned about hard selling the better I became at bending the truth and everyone around me was doing it too so it seemed to be alright, always a great justification for my poor behaviour. I didn't think too much about what I was doing at the time because it was working so I had no incentive to really look at how my actions were affecting my life and the lives of those I was coming into contact with. After a number of years the British economy went into recession and some of the businesses I had sold photocopiers to were going into liquidation.

One of my customers was facing bankruptcy due to her debts. A large part of her debt problem was due to her photocopier contract, as the hidden penalties in the small print were substantial. I met with her and she broke down in front of me. For the first time I understood the impact on others of what I'd been doing. I was horrified that this was the impact of the business I was part of and I didn't know how to deal with the consequences. All I could do was write off her debt so that it became mine. My business was also affected by this and the recession. By the time I was twenty one I owed a large sum of money and my business had collapsed. In retrospect it was the best thing that could have happened to me.

What were some of the big events that have changed your life?

How did you behave, what was your impact and how did it contribute to the situation?

These days I want people to feel safe and supported around me so that they have the space to explore their own solutions to their lives and leadership. I want people to feel challenged too, and that they will be asked to look at and understand the impact of who they are being, even if today feels difficult. I want people to look forward to spending time with me because I am a positive person who helps others see what is possible. I want people to feel cared for and honoured by me.

It is only by being clear on this that we are able to choose our behaviours and bring them to all aspects of our lives. By the way, if I catch someone breaking into my house in the middle of the night, I want them to feel more frightened of me than I am of them!

The impact we have on the world is a choice we can make and we are able to choose that impact at any given moment. In order to do that it is essential that we are clear on the impact that we want to have. In the same way that when we reach a road junction it helps us to be clear which way to turn to get to our chosen destination. Impact manifests in the way others feel around us. Our impact manifests by what is going on around us as it either emboldens and engages others or puts them off and causes problems. What we do affects everyone we come across, how we do it is our choice.

Look at all of the different areas in your life and think about the impact you want to have in them.

What is the impact you want to have in each of the different areas in your life?

How do you want people to feel around you?

What would you like to be possible because of your impact?

What is the impact you would like to have on the people you meet and the world around you?

As you start to choose the impact that you want to have, be guided by your values, beliefs and by what you care about.

The impact we have determines how others experience us. How they experience us then helps to create our reputation.

how does your impact affect you and others?

notes

what reputation do you want to create?

The thing about a reputation is that whether you want one or not, you've got one. Everyone who comes into contact with others has a reputation. You have some reputation with most of the people you've met, and depending on your reputation you'll have one with some people you've never met. Reputation is what is thought or known or said about you by others. Reputation is what precedes you into any room, situation or conversation. Reputation sets others expectations of you and sets them up to look for evidence of you behaving in that way. Reputations are never the whole of us and they affect how people behave with us. An easy way to see how this takes place is to think of three people you know and for each one notice what you would tell others about them, their good points, the things that are irritating about them, what you enjoy about them and what you might need to watch out for. Whatever your answers to these questions they will set the way you approach all of your interactions with this individual. And whatever your answers they will rarely be the whole truth about that person.

Your reputation helps or hinders what you want in your life even when you are not there. People will come to their own conclusions about you without ever talking to you. Your reputation will get you invited or not, it will get you work or offers to be part of something. It will determine how the world interacts with you and it will get in the way of, and even prevent what you want the most.

What do you think your reputation is in the different areas of your life?

How do you know?

Why not ask a few people?

I remember two stories about my reputation very clearly. When I left Unilever to become a leadership consultant I already had a reputation with some of my colleagues. I was known as a bit of a wheeler dealer and a real salesman. Possibly because of my experience of selling photocopiers I was direct and not afraid to ask difficult questions. I was also known to be a bit unconventional, so I'd follow the rules but not always in the conventional manner. I'd stopped lying years ago, I'd learnt that lesson already but I did have a healthy disregard for the accepted way things ought to be done.

Three years later I was asked back to Unilever to coach and mentor with a new leader. I had been on a big journey in the meantime in meeting Diane, becoming a father to two great stepsons, Josh and Roddy, and our own daughter Imogen. I had set up my own business and I was a very different man from the one who used to work there.

Walking through the office to meet my client I was greeted with shouts of 'How you doing mate – still ducking and diving?' People were treating me in the way they remembered me, it was true for them although it was my old reputation. This felt really strange and because that person had grown up and changed, I could barely remember what it was like to be him. It felt as if they were talking to someone else and in a way they were. The next strange experience was sitting down with my new client. We had never met before as he had joined Unilever after I had left but due to my reputation he thought he already knew me. He wanted a chat before we started any work together as he had heard a lot of stories about me and wasn't at all sure if I was the sort of person he really wanted to help him and his team. He wanted someone who was a professional, who could be challenging with him, who would take his issues seriously, who could stand alongside him with integrity and who would treat the conversations as completely confidential. From what he had heard he felt that most of his requirements wouldn't be met. I was shocked, as I had worked hard to be the person he had just described. It meant that I had to work harder than usual in my first meeting because of what he had heard. It did show me in the extreme how a reputation that is often very different from who you really are can have an effect without you even knowing about it. My old reputation had nearly lost me a client and I wasn't even there.

Alternatively a good reputation can transform the world that you live in. In 2005 my colleagues and I started working with a new client. Over the next 12 months we worked with about 300 of their senior leaders and helped them dramatically transform their leadership to the extent that they completely changed the culture of their organisation. The leaders in that company valued us and believed in our approach. They told everyone else who was going to be working with us how great we were and how great our approach was. They told their colleagues about the difference they would make by working with us and that what we did was very powerful. Every piece of work we undertook with that client from thereon was outstanding because people arrived in the mindset of; this is going to be great and we've heard great things about you and so guess what? – It was always great! We had worked hard at ensuring that we had the impact we intended and we had behaved in a way guaranteed to create a great reputation.

Where has your reputation helped you?

Where has it got in the way?

The difference between these two stories is that both reputations were true to an extent. I had been less 'corporate' than most at Unilever, I was unconventional and thought that rules were mainly for guidance rather than strict obedience – I still do. I wasn't consciously creating a reputation back then so it all rather took on a life of its own and became an exaggerated caricature of me. It gave me a lot of work to do and almost prevented me from working with a good client who had never even met me. Without owning my reputation I had allowed it to become potentially dangerous to the life I wanted to lead. In the second story my reputation was great, I brought energy, real passion and enthusiasm to my client but I also had the courage to be the person I really wanted to be. I was using my aspirations to guide me. There was also a danger here too – When people think you're great, enjoy it and do more of whatever you are doing, but never, never believe that it is wholly true. There are dragons in that direction!

When you are living your life on purpose your reputation is something that you own, you design and you take out to the world. So let's start at the beginning, if you are going to have a reputation anyway, what is the reputation you are going to create for yourself? And because it's your reputation you can have anything that you want here. Go on, be bold and imagine something extraordinary.

What would you like people to say about you?

What is the reputation you would like to have?

What would you like this reputation
to create for you?

what reputation do
you want to create?

notes

living on purpose

What is a purpose? I think it can be anything that brings meaning and direction to your life. It doesn't have to be grand and save the world although it can be if that is what you wish. What it does have to do is connect you with the life you want to be living and the person that you want to be. It has to feel right and give you a sense of excitement and energy.

For many years I worked in business and enjoyed what I did, I seemed to be quite good at it and it paid the rent. It didn't always fill me with excitement and I didn't often jump out of bed in the morning full of purpose to embrace the day with, but it earned me money and I knew what I was doing. I'd always had a feeling that there was something else I was meant to be doing, but it wasn't clear and I hadn't found it yet. This changed when I started to develop my leadership through a series of workshops I attended within Unilever. Through these workshops I discovered my own leadership and explored my future and what might be possible for me. During this time I also found that I had an ability to help my colleagues explore their own leadership and futures too. It became very clear that helping others grow and develop as leaders was what I wanted to do in the world. I had never felt so focused before and the energy and inspiration to do this just kept getting stronger and stronger. Eventually I chose to follow my heart and was ready to do something about my future. I told my boss that I was going to resign in 12 months to become a Leadership Consultant. I started to forge links in this area and I prepared to create my new life. I knew what I wanted to do, and changing everything in one go can be very scary and at times the thought of what I was doing terrified me.

As the time got closer and closer, most mornings felt like Christmas as a child. Nervous excitement, anticipation, wide awake and, of course, desperately hoping that I was going to get what I wished for.

Purpose can also be a lot more immediate and doesn't always require a major shift in our lives. Some people choose to feed the birds, pick up litter as they go, donate some of their time to a worthy cause, be a great friend, partner, son, daughter, mother or father. Some choose to pay it forward, make people smile, be fit and healthy, build a family house or write a book. It doesn't matter what you choose as long as it gives you a sense of connection to something that feeds your soul, gives you energy and in some way for you, makes a difference. Purpose is often linked with hope and ambition. Whatever you choose for yours, notice if it gives you either of those.

What could you get excited about?

What gives you a feeling of hope and ambition?

When we look around us we can find so many examples of people who are or were living on purpose. From well known leaders who changed their countries and the world to people from all walks of life who are trying to make a difference. They usually share some similar characteristics. They are focused on a vision of the future, they are committed to achieving it and they are passionate about the difference it will make to them and others. Just about everything you see in the world around you started with someone imagining an idea or dreaming a dream, and then doing something about it.

Who in the world do you admire
who has a sense of purpose?

What are some of their characteristics?

Whatever you choose for your own purpose doesn't have to be forever. You can have more than one purpose and you can change your mind. When you find one that you like, try it out, see if it fits, notice how it makes you feel as you walk through the world with that purpose in your mind. When I was small if someone had asked me 'did you do that on purpose?' it was usually because I had done something wrong. These days, when I'm being who I want to be, I am able to say 'yes, I did'.

Being clear on your purpose provides a signpost and a reminder. It always brings you back to who you want to be and what you want to do. What this doesn't mean is that as soon as it gets tough you can just change your mind. Letting go of any purpose you have chosen for yourself requires a good, long look in the mirror first.

have you ever?

Have you ever seen anything as wonderful
as your own brilliance?
The way you unfold like a flower when inspired
with a purpose beyond your mortality
Has it occurred to you that now is here, and love in each new
moment is as important as the last?
That all thoughts and acts carried with great
love change you and others
And that all thoughts and acts carried without great love
change you and others.

Is there a difference?

Have you ever stood in the presence of the vibrant sunrise at
dawn and felt the first warmth of the day's potential caress
your face, and have you let that touch you?
Have you ever stood on the edge of the world at sunset and
watched the last flare of brilliance at the days end, and have
you let that touch you?
Have you ever seen more possibility than now?

Have you ever turned to face the world and said.

'This is me
I am here
I can be and do what I want
I can change the world today'

And then stepped into it?

I thought I was going to change the world
Maybe I did, or maybe I changed myself
And the world came along for the ride.

I wonder what I will do tomorrow.

Ian Lock

You can discover your purpose in many ways and there are three different approaches in this chapter for you to use. A great way to begin is to picture your life in the future and imagine what you want it to look and be like. This is a powerful way of helping you to dream about what you want for your life. It helps to be in a mindset where everything is possible and you can focus on who you want to be, so take some time to remind yourself of the ground you have covered so far in Being Extraordinary. What follows is a way of meeting your future self and exploring what you would like to be proud of in the future. Treat it as a conversation as you read the questions and prompts, let them spark positive images in your head. You don't need to have answers for them all immediately. See what you can create here and it works whether you explore on your own or with someone who will help and encourage you.

Imagine your life ten years from now. Your life has turned out exactly the way that you have wanted it to. You have lived your life focusing on your values, beliefs and you are spending time on the things you care about. You have worked hard to create the impact and reputation that you have imagined and you have lived those ten years on purpose. Your dreams for the future have become reality and you feel happy. Take some time to imagine what this life is like.

Keep your view of this future in mind.

Where have you made a difference and why was it important to you?

What has your purpose been and how have you felt living on purpose?

I first used this way of imagining my purpose six years ago. When I had finished I looked back over what I had imagined and was quite amazed, possibly even a little daunted by it. One thing was clear, there was a whole lot of future and purpose contained in that list – here is some of it:

1. **My Family**

   My family is healthy, both physically and emotionally. My relationship with my wife is loving, we share our lives and still want to spend the rest of them together. My relationship with my children is strong and full of mutual respect and caring. We are friends as well as family. They come home often and we enjoy our time together. We have the sort of home that people feel welcome in and want to visit.

2. **My Work**

   I am successful and in demand. The work I am doing makes a real difference and I am fulfilled by it. I am able to do this work authentically and with integrity. I work with people who are really making a difference and who are willing to impact the world around them. I work in Whitehall and am helping them to lead more effectively and I work globally with business leaders to help them make their organisations and therefore their worlds a better place. I work with the United Nations helping them bring authentic leadership to all parts of the globe. I work with major sporting organisations helping real leadership develop in these areas – particularly Formula 1 and motor sport. Thirty percent of my work each year is not charged and is with not for profit organisations that are making a big difference.

3. **My Health**

I am fit and healthy and exercise regularly. I have a good diet and I'm really pleased that I've stopped smoking.

4. **My Friends**

I have a close set of friends who I spend quality time with. This gives me a healthy balanced life outside of work and family. I have always helped my friends out when they have needed it and they have always helped me. We do things that make us feel alive.

5. **Financially**

We are financially secure, we have savings and we are not constantly worried about money. I am organised in my financial affairs and know what I am doing.

6. **My Interests**

I have written a book that is accessible to many and has made a difference to those who have read it and helped them have the life that they want. I'm a better driver and have started to take part in a number of regular motor sports events. I have my own race car and compete successfully. I have enjoyed some of the great walks in the world.

7. **Leadership**

The world is a different place because leaders have seen that there is a bigger picture and that life has more to offer than just delivering the bottom line. Leaders are looking at their organisations differently and creating workplaces that are inspiring, fulfilling places to be that deliver extraordinary results. Our world leaders are making a difference to the way people live as they are consistently able to engage with real life and are making choices for the good of us all. I'm proud of this because I have contributed to it.

As I looked through this list I could see that what I had written was very important to me and there was much that would be purposeful. Those that made me feel most uncomfortable to read, or looked too big or difficult for me to achieve, were the ones that I wanted the most. To make this future real I was going to have to be very committed. Six years into my list I'm doing quite well. My family is in great shape, I have a full diary and I am working in Whitehall and across the world. I am mainly working with people who are trying to make a real difference, and I regularly work with not for profit organisations. I am quite healthy, have a good set of friends and I have written a book – which I hope is making a difference as you read it. On the other hand, I am still working on the smoking and I don't yet own my own racing car or compete regularly. I am not financially secure, the world isn't that much of a different place yet and I am ever hopeful, I am not working with the UN and I am not doing any leadership work in sport and motor sport. So there's still quite a lot to go for.

A different way to explore what you want for your purpose is to remember what your childhood dreams were. What did you want to be when you grew up, what did you want to do? It's a great experience to revisit those dreams and look at them again. I often ask people I'm working with this question. For many it takes them back to a time where adult responsibility and lots of good reasons not to do something are replaced by a childlike wonder where anything was possible. Make a list of everything you wanted to be and keep an open mind as to how you might get close to them today. I really, really wanted to be a Formula 1 racing driver, I was possibly not talented enough, rich enough or dedicated enough to make that happen. I did, however in my mid 20's, race pro karts for 10 years with my good friend Rossie, and thoroughly enjoyed it. It wasn't the same as being an F1 driver and it was great, great fun.

What did you want to be when you grew up?

What do you want to be when you grow up?

There is another way to start to unlock the question of our purpose and I've left it until last because it doesn't just refer to us, it's also a great way to understand those around you, your family and friends and people that you spend time with. There are 3 areas for you to explore here

The first area is about what we want. We are often asked this and it's usually in the context of something fairly instant. Here the exploration is deeper than just the instant and is asking us to think about what we really want for us and others in our life. Being clear on what you want in your life helps you to focus and explore how you will make it happen.

The second area to explore is our future success. This is where you describe how 'what you want' looks like, feels like and the difference it has made. Imagine how everything would be in the life that you have imagined when it has turned out the way you wanted it to be.

The third area is where you look at your passion and reasons for making this happen. What it is that excites you and compels you to do it. The word compelling is important here, when something is compelling you just have to do it.

I have found the three questions overleaf a great help to exploring this more.

Have a look at these three questions and
spend some time imagining and thinking
about what your answers could be.

What do you want?

What does success look like for you?

What makes this compelling for you?

Now go and ask the people you care about the
same questions – their answers might surprise you

We can often bring a deep level of seriousness to our own life and our future, and whilst that is sometimes wholly appropriate it is also very healthy to approach these big conversations with a lightness and playfulness that allows us to experiment with what we want. It also helps us be more compassionate with ourselves when we stumble or fall as we try something new. Notice which inner voice you are choosing to listen to as you start to create your purpose. Is it making you small or is it helping you to imagine an extraordinary life?

Take some time, use everything that you've explored throughout this chapter and start to imagine your purpose.

What would you like to change about you, your life and the world that you live in?

What is the difference you want to make?

In your life, what do you want your purpose to be?

Start to complete the following statements..

My Purpose is...

The difference I want to make focusing on my purpose is...

living on purpose

notes

chapter 11

being extraordinary

This is where everything you have imagined and thought about comes together. From this point on you are designing your own guide to living and leading the life that you want. Every choice you make from here will determine how you create and activate your life on purpose. It is about being extraordinary.

We are fantastic. I'm constantly reminded of this whenever I talk to people, especially people who are living with their own sense of purpose and are therefore aware that they need to bring something special to make it happen. For many of us just living the best way that we can or the best way that we can imagine is enough to get us to the future we want. For those of us that are trying to make a much bigger difference just living as best that we can, may not be enough. For some the only way to bring true transformation in their life is by being extraordinary. So what does being extraordinary look like?

It starts with the being. This is not doing extraordinary things, that will come anyway, it is being an extraordinary human being. It is paying close attention to your sense of self and to your future and purpose, it is helping yourself and others to imagine and hold possibilities that were previously unimaginable, it is being conscious of who and how you want to be in everything that you are doing and bringing focus and clarity to the people around you. It is being truly committed to whatever it is you believe in and doing the very best that you can to bring it about. History is full of people who have achieved the impossible, and in some way they have all been extraordinary.

Just the thought that you could be extraordinary requires that you step outside of what is comfortable for you and take the risk that it might not work. If it doesn't work try again and then try it in a different way. If you really believe in what you are doing keep trying until you find a way that works. Being extraordinary rarely comes with a guarantee of safety and success but it usually comes with a guarantee of being truly alive to yourself and the world that you live in. Often the experience of doing something extraordinary or attempting it is enough, the end result is whatever it will be and whatever you can make it. It's often the journey and how we make the journey that is the most extraordinary part. One thing I have learnt is that just by being here today, just by having made it this far in your life, just by living – you are already extraordinary in some way. I have yet to meet anyone who isn't.

Don't measure extraordinary by the end result,
measure it by your sense of purpose, enjoyment
and how alive you feel on the journey.

To truly live the life you want requires real commitment and there is a magic about making that commitment which often transforms everything about and around us.

Until one is committed there is hesitancy,

the chance to draw back – always ineffectiveness.

Concerning all acts of initiative there is one elementary truth,

the ignorance of which kills countless ideas and splendid plans:

That the moment one definitely commits oneself, then

Providence moves too. All sorts of things occur to help one

that would never otherwise have occurred.

A whole stream of events issue from the decision, raising in

one's favour all manner of unforeseen incidents and meetings

and material assistance, which no man could have dreamt

would have come his way.

I have learned a deep respect for one of Goethe's couplets:

'Whatever you can do, or dream you can, begin it.

Boldness has genius, power and magic in it.'

W H Murray, Scottish Himalayan Expedition

practising

The key to creating the life you want is practice. Practice is not about getting it right, it's about practice.

When we are growing up it is accepted that we need to take time to learn and it is even expected for us to make mistakes on the way. Learning our multiplication tables or how to spell and write is a process we go through. Practising how to live in the world is another learning when we are young, and if we're lucky enough to have good parents and teachers we get quite a lot of leeway and encouragement as we find our way through these lessons. As we get older, it's almost as if it's suddenly not alright to take time to learn, we are harsh with ourselves and try not to get things wrong. We expect ourselves and others to grasp new challenges instantly, no matter how difficult they are. This expectation can be even stronger when we set ourselves personal goals and try to change our lives. I remember the utter joy and frustration I experienced about 10 years ago when I started to learn to surf. This was a completely new experience for me and a skill I didn't have. The focus and concentration required was both exhilarating and exhausting. Time and time again I would try to stand up on the board once I had caught a wave and fall headfirst into the water. It took me about 20 hours of practice before I could stand, even briefly, on the board. This was because I refused to take any lessons for the first week as I thought I ought to be able to do it myself!

There were times when my desire to get it right would be so strong that each failure was like a personal indication of my utter inability to be good at surfing. I noticed at the time how the voice in my head would say that surfing was a silly thing and you can't do this, stop it and do something else. My desire not to fail almost stopped me continuing. I also remember the first wave that I rode into shore all the way and the sheer exhilaration that I felt on being able to do it. Hours of practice had paid off, or so I thought. My next mistake was to think that I had mastered it and knew what I was doing. In essence I stopped practising and started 'being a surfer'. Three hours later after heading out deep into the sea to catch the big waves, and not standing up and being completely beaten up by the water, it occurred to me that I needed to pay attention to my continued practice in order to improve or even have any chance of 'being a surfer'. As soon as I thought I knew what I was doing, I stopped practising.

The same applies to living the life that you want, practice is all about paying attention to what we are doing and focusing on the changes that we want to make. When practising Being Extraordinary set yourself targets that are reachable and once you get good at that then stretch yourself further. Traditionally my style has always been to challenge myself to the limit and use that to measure my self-worth. These days I try to be gentler and help myself succeed.

How much time do you give yourself
· to learn something new?

What do you say to yourself as you are learning?

Does it make you more or less likely to succeed?

Self compassion is a large part of practising Being Extraordinary. What do I mean by self compassion?

For me, self compassion is:

- your own ability to love and care for yourself in all of your different ways that you can be in your life.
- being delighted when you manage to be brilliant and, here's the big ask, delighted when you manage to be truly awful.
- allowing yourself to be whatever you are today, this month, this life and not putting yourself down or feeling bad about where you are and what you do.
- embracing all the parts of you that work well and embracing all the parts of you that don't. It's about holding a new form of perfection, that being whoever you are is perfectly you.
- picking yourself up when you fall and acknowledging that you fell, not beating yourself up that you fell.

- embracing the whole of you, the good and the bad, the skilled and the clumsy, the happy and the sad. It's believing that who you are is someone worth knowing.

Self compassion allows you to practise well as it helps you understand and accepts that when you are practising you can get it right or fall down and that both are about the learning and the journey. You know what? We fall down, we do daft things, we say the wrong things, we behave poorly and we get it wrong. We are also able to be truly magnificent, be wonderfully generous, help others and make a positive contribution to the world. It's called being human and our ability to do these things grants us access to a fabulous little club in the Universe called the human race.

We can be both wonderful and terrible within minutes of each other and that is what makes us human. It's allowed.

For most of my life I had not been able to accept the parts of me that were scared, that got it wrong, the parts that struggled, the person who would awkwardly say the wrong thing at the wrong time. I eventually vowed to search this person out from within myself and banish him. Eventually I decided that the only way to do this was to remove fear itself from my life and because my self-compassion was non-existent I gave myself a month to do this. This is the fascinating part of self compassion or a lack of it. I had been living with fear for many years, possibly my whole life and yet I had only given myself a month to rid my psyche of this problem. Of course I had no chance, even if I'd given myself 10 years I would not have made it. It was at this point I was attending a workshop run by the poet David Whyte and he suggested that our only hope lay in embracing those parts of ourselves that we don't like and particularly welcoming in the fear as an important and valuable part of who you are. This suggestion felt preposterous and it transformed the way I saw myself! The thought of embracing these small, weak and unwelcome parts of me was completely foreign and as I explored the idea further I discovered that accepting all of me was the most compassionate thing I could do. It has not been easy and in order to live the life that I want I have had to start practising self compassion.

How will you treat yourself with compassion?

How will you challenge and encourage yourself to be extraordinary?

How will you be kind to yourself when you are not?

You wait a lifetime to meet someone who understands you and accepts you as you are. At the end, you find all along, that someone, has been you.

Richard Bach

One of the best ways of creating a change in your life is to keep being conscious of what you are practising. The best place to begin is in the morning so that you have the rest of the day to bring it to life. At the start of the day, without being conscious of it we can easily move into a mode where we are thinking about all of the tasks we have to do that day or start being excited, worried or concerned about what lies ahead. Some of us make lists in our heads of all the things that we need to do and others of us start to plan the day and think about what is happening. How do you start your day?

A while ago I was asked to speak at a conference in Whitehall, London. I'd been given 10 minutes to engage a large group of senior civil servants on the topic of leadership. This felt very challenging and had been filling me with apprehension for weeks before. As the day approached, that apprehension started to turn into fear and my head became full of all the ways that I could fail at this and I had stopped sleeping properly. I even scripted the 10 minute slot so that I could just read it straight out – something I never ever do! I'd planned the night before to try to wake up in the morning and think of why I was doing this, how it fitted in with my purpose and the difference I wanted to make. As I went through my usual morning routine I focused on who I wanted to be and what my purpose was today. By the time I arrived in London I was still nervous and I was also clear on my reasons for being there. Two minutes before I was announced on stage I threw away my prepared notes and was ready to be me and be spontaneous in my preferred style. The feedback was that it made a big impact and got people thinking. I didn't cover all that I'd scripted but they got a much more authentic and involved me because I was able to hold on to why I was there and I really enjoyed it. I do notice that the times I struggle are usually when I have not been in touch with my core and my purpose.

What will you choose to focus on
at the start of the day?

Have a think about some of the events that you are approaching in your life. Which are the important ones to you and how might you use the person that you've explored and described in this book to make them extraordinary? It might be an important conversation, the start of a new phase of your life, a job interview or a weekend away. Whatever you think of, note a couple of them down and start to think about how you could use what you've explored in this book to make it extraordinary? How could you be there at your best and living on purpose? What difference would it make if you were paying close attention to your impact and purpose? How would you be in these situations and how would you handle things? That's the big help, that last question, ask it of yourself as often as you can remember to – What would you at your best, standing for your values and beliefs, do right now? How would you handle this?

notes

your guide to an extraordinary life

The guide that you create for yourself here will have a huge influence on the life that you want to lead.

Being Extraordinary is being bold, daring to go for the life that you want. It is believing in who you are and who you could be and having the courage to be more than you ever thought you could.

Use the framework overleaf to focus your hopes and dreams for your future. Be bold and be adventurous. Make it enjoyable and make it purposeful. Create a guide that will give you the life that you have always wanted, a guide that will give you the ability to shape your world.

Play with it, have fun with it and make it work for you.

Practice is different for each of us and we all have different ways of applying it. This is what I do to make this work and keep it simple:

1. Choose who you want to be, and write it down.

2. Choose what you want to believe about you, others and the world that you live in, and write it down.

3. Choose the impact and reputation you want in the world, and write it down.

4. Choose the purpose you want and describe the life you want to live, and write it down.

5. Be clear on what and how you are going to practise for 28 days and the difference that will make to your life, and write it down.

---

6. Ask yourself everyday 'What would you at your extraordinary best, do now?

7. Share what you are practising with others and ask for their help.

8. Read your guide to an extraordinary life everyday for the next 28 days (and beyond) at the start of each day and apply it to everything you are going to be doing and the life you are creating.

9. Celebrate your successes and failures with equal satisfaction because being extraordinary is about the journey and the trying, not the result. If some things you are trying don't work, pay attention as to why and try again. You always have another chance. The things that do work – remind yourself that it was you that made it work.

10. Retain a sense of humour, perspective and compassion as you go and remember to enjoy. This is about the rest of your life so why wouldn't you?

What you choose to do with everything you have created from here is truly down to you. I don't know what life you are living or what your hopes and ambitions are for the future. I don't know how you arrived at this point in your life. I do hope that whatever the answers, you move forward with a great sense of direction and purpose, heeled over with the wind and spray of life in your face, setting a true course for the future with a smile or at least a look of excited determination and that you really enjoy the journey to wherever you are headed. Keep looking, keep questioning, keep choosing, keep being extraordinary and enjoy living the rest of your life on purpose.

living on purpose

There is a fierce purpose buried deep within ourselves
The knowledge of which we have long kept hidden
What is precious to us does not care to be recognised.
Listen to the silence
and hear the voice of your true self speaking urgently
from the depths
Catch the open gate and walk through
Embracing the gift that is truly yours
Revel in the vulnerability that certain uncertainty brings
Accept the humiliation that comes with
an astonishing newness
And return to the ground of your being.

Find the new voice
Find the spark
Embrace your purpose
Plot your course and follow your heart
Living, living, living at last.

Ian Lock

being extraordinary

notes

keep in touch

Much of our learning in this world comes from those around us, people from everyday life that we meet. There is fantastic help and information out there for us all. If we can only connect ourselves to others who are living their life on purpose then there is the possibility for great learning. If you want to know more about Being Extraordinary visit the website www.being-extraordinary.com and help to create an online community of people who want to make a difference. There will be a blog running and a regular posting so you can sign up and receive new ideas, prompts and stories on Being Extraordinary.

Do share any experiences that you have – what's working for you, what isn't, what you have learnt, how you are practising, stories about you and others being extraordinary. Whatever you want to say you can do it by sending an email or post to connect@being-extraordinary.com and we'll look to publish as many as we can on the site. You can also visit the Facebook page

Being Extraordinary and follow us and others @beingextra on Twitter where you can tweet your own experiences and observations of making a difference or things that have inspired you. Your experience might just be that little bit of gold that someone else is looking for.

acknowledgements

Writing this book has been an incredible experience. It would not have been possible without the help, support and critical input of many people.

I would like to thank my friend and editor, Anni Townend, for her support throughout, walks along the downs, many cups of tea, for finding a publisher and for editing this book in a way that was both critical and, importantly for a first time author, very encouraging.

I am indebted to my test readers who gave up their time and were willing to tell me what they thought and suggest where I wasn't hitting the spot for them, especially as they knew I was nervous about hearing their comments. I did listen to all of the feedback and it all really helped. So thank you to John Connor, Lucy Kidd and Anthony Landale for your great insights and encouragement.

A special mention for Jo Wynn who not only read the book and provided feedback, she also spent 12 hours reading my book aloud to me so I could hear what I had written and more importantly where it wasn't working.

Also for telling me all those years ago to be quiet and listen to what others had to say, I did and she was right.

To Steve Radcliffe my friend and mentor of many years. It was a long time ago that Steve took a risk with me, an untried and untested consultant, and brought me into one of his clients. Without Steve's encouragement and guidance over the years this would have been a very different, and probably lesser book. Without his prompt to look ten years into the future I would never have imagined this was possible.

To Josh and Roddy, my sons. Josh for reading the manuscript at a crucial time for me, giving me important feedback and telling me he loved it and for his invaluable input and expertise on digital marketing. Roddy for offering to create the website and involve his mates at University to come up with something quite incredible.

To Immi, my daughter, for getting published before me – many times, and just being there and being special.

My Mum, for reading through the manuscript, sitting down with me and reminding me how to spell practice, and the difference between effect and affect.

And for bringing back memories, for a brief and wonderful moment, of what it was like to be young again and having my homework checked!

Murielle Maupoint of Live It Publishing, who loved the idea, loved the book, and had real energy and enthusiasm to be involved and to publish my writing from the outset.

David Whyte for his words, particularly on fear and for 'What to remember upon waking' that set me up to start the day very differently.

A huge thank you to my family who have had to put up with me being engrossed and consumed by this book and have borne it mainly with great encouragement and good grace. Most importantly thank you to Diane, who has read the book more times than I or she cares to mention and has unfailingly been supportive all the way through. Without her I would have never started this in the first place and would not have had the strength and courage to go this far.

Ian Lock – July 2012

about the author

Photograph by Chris Taylor

Ian Lock lives with his family in East Sussex in a small village close to the beautiful South Downs.

Since 1999 he has been a leadership consultant to organisations around the world helping them transform the impact of their leadership and the energy of their people. He runs Ian Lock Associates Ltd and is also a core member of the team at Steve Radcliffe Associates.

He is passionate about leadership and the difference that it can make to the world in any and every walk of life.

He believes that anyone, whoever they are, can be extraordinary and probably already are.

www.being-extraordinary.com

what's it like
working with ian?

"Ian and I worked together over a period of about 5 years unleashing new and different possibilities with many colleagues from the retail team. We did lots of great stuff together in building a new culture and bringing together new teams. The essence of every conversation Ian worked with us was about one thing and that was building the level of belief and most importantly confidence required to achieve personal and team breakthroughs. As a result of the conversations which started happening everywhere, more of the team started to show up in their most special way… simply but very powerfully just ready to be much more of themselves.

Ian is a great guy to spend time with… He listens brilliantly and really understands what it will take for individuals and teams to get back in touch… and stay in touch with what makes them special.

He brings people together and helps them discover the way through on what can seem impossible… so that afterwards everyone is thinking that was no problem and with my new found confidence anything becomes possible."

Simon Roberts, COO, Boots UK

"I first got to know Ian and his work through working with him as a coach but this turned into an enormous personal journey for myself and our senior team. Ian has a special quality that enables an individual to truly reflect on what they stand for, believe in and aspire to be. It is only then that they can discover the greatness that is within."

Julie MacDonald, HR Director, Pizza Express

"*Being Extraordinary* translates Ian Lock's unparalleled approach to helping people unlock their own values, beliefs and what they truly care about, and have them determine for themselves their real purpose in life. As I personally experienced with 2 different management teams, Ian's method is both simple and accessible by all.

At a more personal level, Ian's contribution has been in helping me to sharpen the impact I want to have on people and how I want them to feel, day in day out."

Stéphane Jacqmin GM

(Unilever, Danone, Reckitt Benckiser)

"I've worked with Ian over the last 7 years within numerous teams to unlock potential and change culture – each time this has led to a real change in delivery for customers. On a personal level, Ian fundamentally helped me understand what was important to me in life, both at work and more importantly at home. Put simply, working together I've become more confident in being myself."

Jonathan Gardner, Divisional Director, Boots UK

"Ian has been an important part of our team's transformation. Almost immediately Ian was able to focus the Senior Team on areas that really mattered. By getting us to look inside ourselves and be honest about our own weaknesses and the larger team issues, he was able to help us chart a course to becoming a more successful, high performing team. He really got to know us and was able to push all the right buttons to get the big stuff out on the table. In addition, the work we did with Ian helped us develop the right framework for moving ahead from a position of strength."

Susie Balch,

Director of Development, London Business School

"I have worked with Ian for the last 10 years and he has helped me come to appreciate that there is no perfect formula for life or leadership: it's about getting in touch with who you are and what you want and then reveling in this, your own, greatness. His insightful framing of the way to consider things has helped me grow. I would strongly encourage anyone sitting there thinking ' is this as good as life gets?' to work with Ian."

Emma Woods, Marketing Director, Pizza Express

"Ian has the ability to make sense out of "stuff that you thought you already knew but weren't really using properly". Working with him hasn't been about learning a big new theory or having to embrace the latest idea in management thinking – instead it's been about re-ordering thoughts, making sense of what you already knew, being clear about where you're going and knowing what you need to do to get there. Supposedly, it's very simple – surprisingly, it's very effective."

Neil Jones, CEO, Make A Wish UK

"Ian Lock is one of the most powerful and distinctive voices currently around in the area of personal leadership. Most of his work is in big organisations where he works with CEOs, directors and executive teams. But he also works with all who have a thirst for change, for anyone who wants to make a difference in their life and, most of all, for anyone who wants to live a more purposeful life. As someone who has worked with Ian I am continually wowed by his insights, coaching and the journeys he takes people on. If you are up for it then get on and enjoy the ride."

Anthony Landale

Much of my work over the last 12 years has been inside of Steve Radcliffe Associates and his ground breaking Future Engage Deliver (www.futureengagedeliver.com) approach to leadership. Steve has created a unique platform that has enabled a powerful and lasting shift in the way leadership is now seen in organisations and a great platform for those of us who work with him to fly from. The endorsements from Boots UK are from my work with Steve Radcliffe Associates and the Future Engage Deliver programme.

DEVASTATED BY REDUNDANCY?

LEARN HOW TO USE THIS OPPORTUNITY TO CREATE A NEW AND BETTER LIFE FOR YOURSELF...

If you're one of the millions either already - or about to be - affected by redundancy, this book is for you.

It will enable you to:

- walk away from negative feelings of loss, despair, sadness;
- Understand that your occupational identity may be a thing of the past, but your unique identity isn't;
- Find the resources you need in this time of transition;
- Identify your new niche in life; and
- Develop positive and powerful ways of achieving it.

**'This book is the next best thing to being coached by Elaine.
On Masterchef, contestants sometimes say "That's me on a plate".
This is Elaine in a book: warm, wise and witty. Best of all, parts of
the book are laugh out loud funny - and I wasn't expecting that.'**
Redundancy coaching client

ISBN: 978-1-906954-55-0   Format: Paperback
Published: 16 October 2012   RRP: £18.99

Despite following the advice of a wealth of best-selling self-help books, most of us still struggle to understand the fundamental laws and principles that govern the universe, our interactions within it and our ability to achieve success, health, wealth and happiness.

Have you ever wondered why the Law of Attraction doesn't work for you?

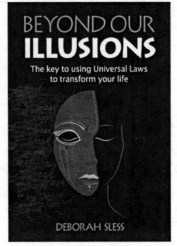

BEYOND OUR
ILLUSIONS
The key to using Universal Laws
to transform your life

DEBORAH SLESS

The answer is simple: The Universal Laws cannot *work in your favour until you identify and remove the psychological issues that are blocking your ability to live the life you want.*

In her ground breaking and easy-to-understand book, psychotherapist Deborah Sless, uses the concrete psychological theory of Transactional Analysis to uncover the secrets of the Universal Laws. **Beyond Our Illusions** takes you on a journey of self-discovery to understand:

- The Universal Laws and how they impact our lives
- Your own individual Life Story and the beliefs that were formed in childhood
- How to achieve freedom from your illusions and master your self
- The concept of Spirit as an energy force and how to tap into it

Genuine self-development is not easy but Deborah Sless provides her readers with the tools and framework they need - through clear explanations, examples and exercises - to begin a journey of self-discovery and change toward ultimate fulfilment.

ISBN: 978-1-906954-42-0
Publication: 1 August 2012

Format: Paperback
RRP: £14.99